HAL•LEONARD
INSTRUMENTAL
PLAY-ALONG

ALTO SAX

AUDIO
ACCESS
INCLUDED

LIZZO
CUZ I LOVE YOU

PLAYBACK+
Speed • Pitch • Balance • Loop

Audio arrangements by Peter Deneff

To access audio visit:
www.halleonard.com/mylibrary

Enter Code
8355-9974-0122-0661

ISBN 978-1-5400-8190-2

HAL•LEONARD®

Visit Hal Leonard Online at
www.halleonard.com

Contact us:
Hal Leonard
7777 West Bluemound Road
Milwaukee, WI 53213
Email: info@halleonard.com

In Europe, contact:
Hal Leonard Europe Limited
42 Wigmore Street
Marylebone, London, W1U 2RN
Email: info@halleonardeurope.com

In Australia, contact:
Hal Leonard Australia Pty. Ltd.
4 Lentara Court
Cheltenham, Victoria, 3192 Australia
Email: info@halleonard.com.au

BETTER IN COLOR

ALTO SAX

Words and Music by LIZZO,
TREVOR DAVID BROWN, WILLIAM ZAIR SIMMONS,
WARREN FELDER and MICHAEL POLLACK

CRYBABY

ALTO SAX

Words and Music by LIZZO,
ERIC FREDERIC, NATE MERCEREAU
and CHARLES HINSHAW

CUZ I LOVE YOU

ALTO SAX

Words and Music by LIZZO,
SAMUEL HARRIS, CASEY HARRIS,
ADAM LEVIN and RUSSELL FLYNN

EXACTLY HOW I FEEL

ALTO SAX

Words and Music by LIZZO,
THERON MAKIEL THOMAS and MICHAEL SABATH

HEAVEN HELP ME

ALTO SAX

Words and Music by LIZZO,
SAMUEL HARRIS, CASEY HARRIS,
and ADAM LEVIN

JEROME

ALTO SAX

Words and Music by LIZZO,
SAMUEL HARRIS, CASEY HARRIS,
and ADAM LEVIN

JUICE

ALTO SAX

Words and Music by LIZZO,
THERON MAKIEL THOMAS, ERIC FREDERIC,
SEAN SMALL and SAM SUMSER

To Coda

D.S. al Coda

CODA

LIKE A GIRL

ALTO SAX

Words and Music by LIZZO,
SEAN DOUGLAS and WARREN FELDER

LINGERIE

ALTO SAX

Words and Music by LIZZO,
THERON MAKIEL THOMAS, ERIC FREDERIC
and NATE MERCEREAU

SOULMATE

ALTO SAX

Words and Music by LIZZO,
SEAN DOUGLAS and WARREN FELDER

TEMPO

ALTO SAX

Words and Music by LIZZO,
THERON MAKIEL THOMAS, ANTONIO CUNA,
MELISSA A. ELLIOTT, DAN FARBER,
ERIC FREDERIC, RAYMOND SCOTT
and ERIC TOBIAS WINCORN

TRUTH HURTS

ALTO SAX

Words and Music by LIZZO,
ERIC FREDERIC, JESSE ST. JOHN GELLER
and STEVEN CHEUNG